If You Are A Kid Straight Out Of Philly

Written by **Brenda Amanda Mwaya**

Illustrated by **Courtney Williamson**

Pucchie Creations
PUBLISHING HOUSE

Dedicated to: J.P.B & J.J.B, Princess Aanya "Dadawaii" V-M
and Princess Caroline "Lina" James S.
You are the Epitome of my Philly Kids! I Love You.

If You Are A Kid Straight Out Of Philly, you will always be a kid at heart!
Everyday is a day to explore.

It's great to be a kid straight out of Philly. Philadelphia is the city of brotherly and sisterly love. Seven days that make a week for you to have fun, fun, fun! Monday, Tuesday, Wednesday, Thursday, Friday, Saturday, all the way to Sunday.

ZOO

Seven days of the week
you are on the go.
Whether it be in The Air
Balloon of the Philadelphia
Zoo, or on a regular Bike,
or on the Double Decker
Bus to see Philly from
another view.

On a Horse Drawn Carriage Ride
in the Beautiful City of Philadelphia.

There are so many ways to get to
all your favorite places!

The Septa Bus,
The Septa Shuttle
Bus, The Septa El Train,
The Septa Orange Line, The
Septa Trolley, The Septa Phlash Bus,
The Stroller or just in the car with
your caregiver, whomever that may be!

Philly is for families! It does not matter whether you
are a baby, a kid, a young adult or a grown up! There are always so
many things to see and places to go. Things to do, do, do!

From the month of January, February, March, April, May, June, July, August, September, October, November all the way to December! Twelve months that make a year!

Morning ☀

☀ Noon

Night 🌙

SNACK · NAP · FUN

From Morning Time, Noon Time, Lunch Time, Nap Time, Snack Time, Play Time to Night Time, Philadelphia's clock does not stop. Philly is busy and on the go! Philadelphia is Philly indeed! Loads of things to do, do, do! Home is only for sleeping. Whether you live outside the city or within the city!

Philly with its food galore!
Found in street corner
stores selling yummy foods to
quiet the rumblings in your tummy! From Cheesesteaks, Cheesecakes, Cold Sandwiches, Falafel, French Fries, Frozen Yogurt, Fruit Salads, Gelato, Hoagies, Hot Dogs, Hot Sandwiches, Ice Cream, Pizza Pies, Pretzels, Water Ice and Snack Bars to Veggie Sticks, just to nibble a few! Let's not forget some Hot Macaroni and Cheese on the go!

Yummy, yummy, ten times yummy! A Philly kid eats on the go! How come
you may ask? Recreational parks with Picnic Tables and so forth.
You can spy them here and there. Playgrounds were created for a kid in Philly!

Four Seasons of the
year for a Philly kid to explore!
From the month of March 1st, all April to May 31st,
three months that make Springtime.
From the month of June 1st, all July to August 31st, three months
that make Summer.

From the month of September 1st, all October to November 30th, three months that make Autumn. From the month of December 1st, All January to February 28th and in some years they have an extra day making 29th of February.

A Leap Year and it ends Winter season. 365 days make a year. 366 days make a Leap Year!

An endless expose of fun to partake, take, take! The City Hall outdoors has The Ice Skating Rink in Winter for that fearless energetic kid in Philly!

At times, a Philly kid is found on a dance floor of The Nest, grooving to the lively tunes of that electrifying One, Mr. Kelvis' voice and a guitar in his hand. One musically seasoned fella everyone must hear!

There is one wonderfully peculiar reader like no other! A Capsule in Time that seriously engages kids from 0 to 5. Lost in the moment due to her captivating ways of story reading! Her faithful young friends listen attentively every mid-Tuesday morning seated all around her like bees to a hive. A kid in Philly has not yet escaped out of that Library without shaking their sillies out on the dance floor leaping energetically to "Five Little Monkeys Jumping On The Bed!"

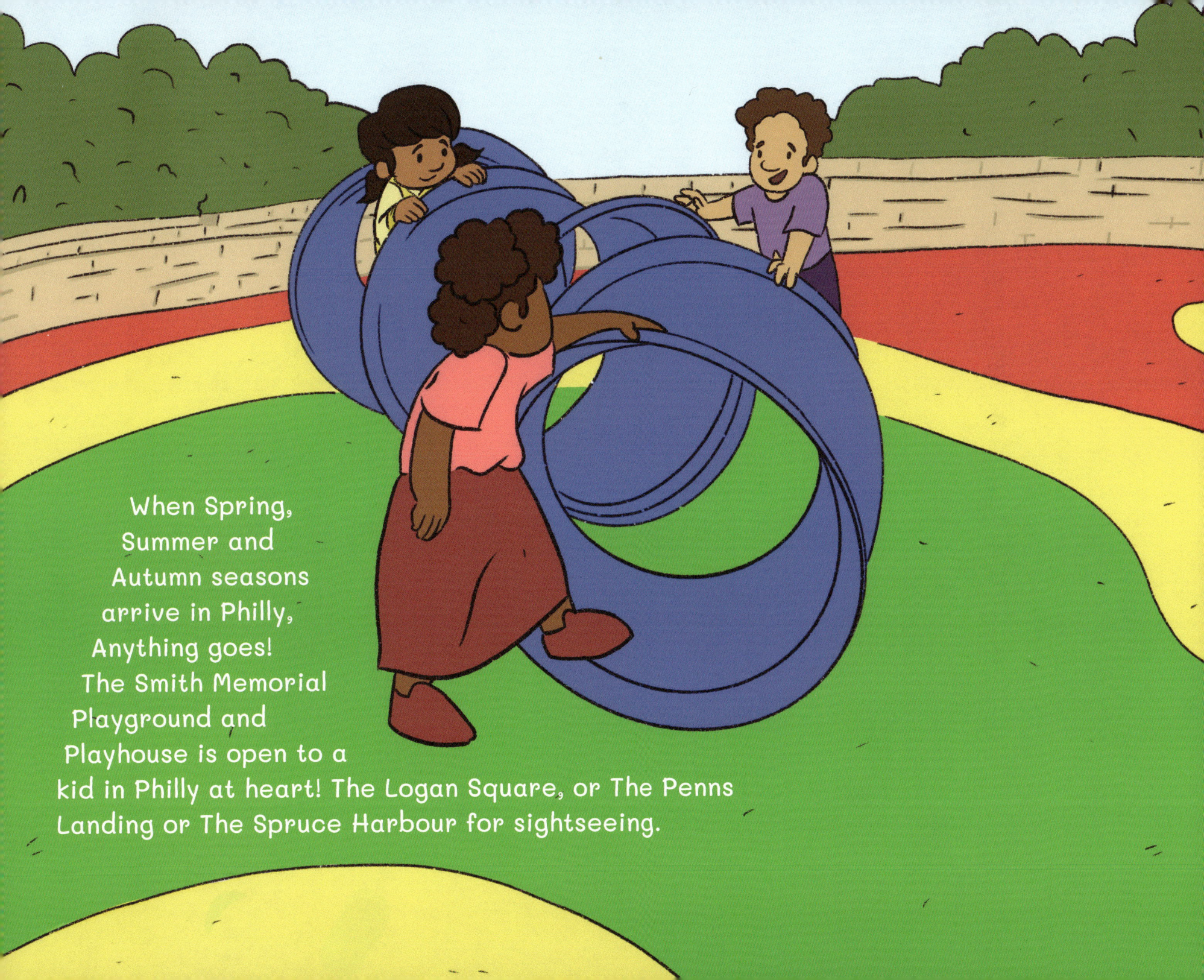

When Spring,
Summer and
Autumn seasons
arrive in Philly,
Anything goes!
The Smith Memorial
Playground and
Playhouse is open to a
kid in Philly at heart! The Logan Square, or The Penns
Landing or The Spruce Harbour for sightseeing.

The Liberty Bell is a great site to see!

The Clean Public Swimming Pools are open to all, especially for that kid who loves water like a fish!

Have you
ever tried
the City Hall
Water Sprinklers?
Loads of fun, fun, fun for the Young and Old.

A family can be spotted outdoors playing with a pet, sometimes!

If you like the smell of barbecue, then family, friends, and neighbors gather up for that hickory smoke barbecue taste of Philly Steak in the evenings and on weekends! Oh, by the way, your pet is invited too.

What about the Arts, you may say!
Broad Street in the heart of
Philly is the place for that.

A kid in Philly can
become a singer,
an actor, a dancer, a
writer, or any artist one
can possibly think of!
Imagination lives, thrives, in Philly!
Imagination comes alive in Philly!

Walking to many places in Philly is fun to do!
Walking around the neighborhood streets gets
a kid to spot a baseball game, or a basketball
game, or a Lacrosse game, or football practice
as well as soccer practice here and there!
A kid straight out of Philly has
no boring moment really!

Too many fun things to do all the day long!

Let's face it, there is nothing better out there than being a kid straight out of Philly! Just imagine If You Were A Kid Straight Out Of Philly in Philly!

There's no telling what you couldn't accomplish in a day!

Brenda Amanda Mwaya is a native of Malawi. A mother to four beautiful children. A designer, inventor and patent holder. In September of 2019, Brenda published her first non-fiction book *An Illegal Immigrant's Journey: How America Became My Destiny*. She also works as a professional nanny in Philadelphia.

Courtney Williamson was born and raised in Philadelphia. From a young age, art had always been a part of her life. So naturally, after graduating from The Philadelphia High School for Creative and Performing Arts, she decided to continue to pursue her love of comics and cartoons, graduating from Moore College of Art and Design in 2014 with a B.F.A in Illustration. She currently works as a free-lance artist in Philadelphia.

CPSIA information can be obtained at www.ICGtesting.com
Printed in the USA
BVIW121909230120
570329BV00006B/15